The Boy with a Sledgehammer for a Heart

poems by

Lex Bobrow

Finishing Line Press
Georgetown, Kentucky

The Boy with a Sledgehammer for a Heart

ACKNOWLEDGMENTS

"A History of Brief Time" was previously published in *Black Heart Magazine*.

"Cure for Chronic Childish," "Cure for Someone Else's Definition of Masculinity,"
and "Cure for Several Ailments, Including Perhaps Loneliness" were previously
published in *Maudlin House*.

"The Asthmatic Boy Learns to Breathe Underwater" and "Every Time You Try
to Live in the Sea, You End Up Back on the Shore" were previously published in
Hermeneutic Chaos.

Publisher: Leah Maines

Editor: Christen Kincaid

Cover Art: Aundre Larrow

Author Photo: Lex Bobrow

Cover Design: Elizabeth Maines

Printed in the USA on acid-free paper.
Order online: www.finishinglinepress.com
        also available on amazon.com

Author inquiries and mail orders:
Finishing Line Press
P. O. Box 1626
Georgetown, Kentucky 40324
U. S. A.

Table of Contents

*For those who have felt
the sledgehammer heart—
and stayed.*

Over Dinner, Reader, We Recite Names of Spells, but Not the Spells Themselves

We name the places our hearts went.
Yours, dissolved into his marvelous dragon breath,
and mine, sunk into her dormant gold aquifer.
We never speak of retrieval.
We cannot take hearts as large as ours back.

Every night, we try to cook into our food
the dusty remnants of our pulverization,
but they condense into the hardest seeds.
After a cracked tooth or two,
we rinse the seeds, save them in jars
stacked along shelves multiplying
in the mirrors we made this house out of.
There's only so much room in the garden.
(Your first crop yielded a matchbook.
Mine, the head of a sledgehammer
like a cabbage, long handle like the roots.
That night, you made the fire, and I the kimchi.
We swallowed our second hearts into place.)

After dinner, in the garden, we name the future,
what kinds of hearts we might grow:
planets, pomegranates, protagonists
of very sad video games.
We name the hours of sleep we won't get:
1:00 AM the Vinyl Hour,
4:00 AM the Hour of Thor's Sweat,
5:00 AM the Hour the Sun Terrorizes Us to Sleep.
We name the book of names we'll compile,
changing its title every night,
the lightyears contained ever-expanding,
the shape of absence barely nameable.

A History of Brief Time

We met with your ship's hull carved into my back.
I, the sea's most ancient shiver of basking sharks,
each ribbed abyss-mouth its own universe
resonating to the terrifying brim with a song
a universe can only birth after eons,
and you, lady, the sailor, deft and hard,
your broad-shouldered heart a monsoon-hammer
on my waters. I felt it, thunderous, in each shark,
each fin and gill pulse—breath, strike, breath.

A storm saw a lover in you, and came barreling
across the ocean, your typhoon heart exactly its type.
I tried to keep it at bay, but the storm wanted you
almost as much as I did, and with tendril winds,
bladed rain, avaricious wave-churn, it knocked you overboard.
(In honesty, I ache for storms—
they do not know how to talk to girls, all roar and batter.)
I caught you, my Jonah, my darling,
with one of my universes. This maw, the best
of all possible worlds: I am human, you are human.

We met with your ship docked at my seaside town.
I, a boy or girl of seventeen, slender as the sometimes moon,
knew even through the Sunday expanse of crystalline sanctuary air,
that you, lady, were a sailor, deft and hard.
You wanted to fuck me after the service, and I wanted
you to fuck me, too, but I said no—not yet.
I let you kiss me in the street markets, by the apples,
the swords, the shark fins. I let you fall in love
with my lips only, and for a week, you loved them well,
but then you were out to sea. I knew you'd come back
to fuck me. It was all you wanted in this whole universe—
to taste every inch of the moon, this sea of crises,
the sweet lunar gift beneath my center of gravity.

Yet you needed the ocean, and here, I had no fins, no gills
to be with you in your need. I waited a lifetime,
and then one more just to be sure,
                                    but you never came back.
I spent the next lifetime learning to sail,
and in the next one, I became the king's favorite admiral.
I made him start war on war on war on war,
stretching the navy to an atom's width to find you,
eternal mariner, failed mouth-chaser, runaway.

And even after scarring the world over with war,
I still hadn't found you.
                          I waited two lifetimes for the world
to heal, all the while studying the ocean. In the second, I married
a shark expert, learned everything about basking sharks.
We had beautiful children who fell in love with the sea
and became sailors (I pretended they were yours).
I told them our story like a creation myth and hoped
they believed it just enough for them to look for you
out on the water. When we all died,

I spent the next lifetime tracking down this world's shiver.
Right at the end, feeble and fragile, I found it and jumped
into a mouth. I found myself the sea, in all its ancient gravity.
I would find you, ever-sailor. You would love me
in this world as you hadn't in any other. So I waited.
With every minute swirl of tide and current, I waited.
I had every single shred of plankton searching
for the bludgeon of your hull on my unrelenting surface.
I counted the (43,800) days until a long human life had passed,
but I could not find you. I could not find you. I even waited
until every living thing in the ocean had been replaced by its child.
I was a new ocean, and yet I had nothing, no hope.
This was the worst of all possible worlds:
I, the sea; you, not a sailor.

I asked the basking sharks to take me to another world,
but they said it would take until the end of time
to filter my being from the ocean. I ordered them to do it.

Day after day, the basking sharks tore me from my body
in granules smaller than sand, storing bits of me in their filters.
The sun began to dim as they were halfway through.
Boats, all the more infrequent, grew sharper hulls
as the waters became denser and more unyielding
(it is the sea's benevolence that allows human travel,
and can benevolence exist without consciousness?)
and I awaited the end of time as every aspect of me was torn.

As the sharks were nearly done, we began to feel it:
the prodigious gravity of the true ending
like so many pulling hands across the bed of the universe.
I urged them onward, onward as space-time drew to a close.
But I knew. We'd meet at the singularity, where everything breaks down—
laws, science, love. Where everything becomes the blood and earwax
of the universe, all in a single point of infinite density.

Fenrir

I.

This night has lasted a year,
and you are January and skybreak,
the relieving of year's end pressure.

Your lips taste like honeydew and forgotten
acquaintances. Cruel Decembers fall
from my mind-sky. I almost forget you,

even as you make me resolve to speak less
and use my tongue more often, to touch
your body with the severe ought that it deserves.

So over you I stand, bare and insufficient
in this, the raw brightness of night.
This rib cage is only valleys.

When I go down, I imagine
I am Odin, drinking deep from the Well,
and I know you—I want to know you.

You leave blueprints on my tongue:
how to build a world in a primeval gap
from the corpse of a giant I have killed.

But I have no world to build away from you,
no slain but the Father of the Slain,
though you have nine worlds away from me.

II.

My blue watercolored lips I use
to paint a river they call "Hope"
from your neck down, down
between your hills to Glitnir
(I played near its walls of red gold
as a pup in Asgard, but I am grown,
and you hold a new Glitnir low,
granting me access every night).
They say a sword locked my mouth open
and my saliva ran free to form that river,
but lady, you are the mouth of these waters.
In this Fimbulwinter room
(we only make love in the cold),
the river freezes over and I am on thin ice.
I am always on thin ice.
The heat of your writhing
cracks the crisp film, melting
it into venomous drops
that drip down to my lips and blacken
my veins. Three winters freeze it again
and you melt it—freeze and melt
and freeze and melt, like something
out of a Norse creation story.
Our story, of course, is the opposite:
I am trying to eat at the bottom of a river.

Running from Fire

I mixed my own bones into the wall.
Everyone you love is a fool, you know.
It doesn't matter. I have become mortar.
Don't make me laugh. You are just
earth-sludge, infatuated. A rancid stone.
I'll drink rotten waterfalls if I have to,
sleep in a bed of blood clots if I have to.
I'll mix my occipital lobe in
with the painkillers, the soup if I have to.
Ah, ever the noble salad. Knighthood is wasted
on the medieval, eh? Gallantry belongs
to the fences, the boulders, the shields.
Does your tongue always taste like a boot?
Only during hurricane season.
And when you indulge in future conditionals.
Love is a rock. *We both know we have no idea*
what that actually means. Stop, listen.
The clouds are singing. *They're screaming,*
"Rain, rain, go away and never come back."
How selfless. They are made of rain.
They're just scared. They'd rather not exist
where they are fathers and mothers of erosion.
I'll be like them if I have to. *There you go again.*
This is what life is about. *We are arsonists at heart.*
Here, in the gravel of my abdomen, in the long bow
of my spine firing stones into the sea, in the sweet
breeze of wheat from my chest, I see it.
Everyone you love is a fool, you know,
a goddamn beautiful fool. *You're going to end up*
an eclipse-ring of juice at the bottom of a cup.
I dream of it. It is a better fate than ashes.

Gravitational Break-Up Poem

I. Baggage

I was always putting out candles.
Now I am all burnt fingertip and marginalia.
I am a thought of ice in the warmest hands.
I am spending too much time insisting "I am."

I had always meant to be an orchard: all blossom, every fruit.
I didn't know I was never meant to taste
like a peach or a honeydew or an apple.
I didn't know I was never made of seeds.

The arsonist licks her fingers
while a lullaby chokes me to death.
Look what she turned me into, what lesson she began.
That is, there is a universal law everyone is afraid to acknowledge:

no one will ever love you exactly the way you want them to.

II. Cardiology

I had hoped it would be the arsonist with her matchbox phone calls
or the assassin with her sugared, avocado lips
or you, the mermaid with your love as pure as the sea.

It's okay. There is exegesis, a glimpse of God in the memory of your kiss,
even though still my moon-tongue pulls at the tides,
still geode exists in place of a beating heart.

A heart is an apple,
and a swiftly broken heart is a plate of apple wedges,
but when was the last time this heart was an apple and not a geode?

III. Metamorphosis

Darling, your slow hands split this sapphire open,
and I am beautiful, more beautiful than any apple.
I cannot rot. I am the starlight gut of the Earth,

a comet's tail of titanium-braced aluminum oxide (and you are my comet).
If you are afraid of floating away, know this:
the crystals you freed are taking over my body,

and now I grow.
This jagged unrelent plants itself deep into the Earth,
then reaches. I reach and twist toward the sky. Beyond it.

Braids of sapphire climb the atmosphere, refracting
sun- and moon- and you-light to shine
on first dates and graves and the fear and the fear.

This stem bulbs and blooms into a new blue moon.
If you are afraid of floating away, know this:
I am massive, and my love is the law of gravity.

Lists of Words to Mouth during a First Kiss with

I. a Stranger at a Party

inveigh, indelible, aloe, spew
repudiate, honeydew, ghoul, willow,
choose, quake, spew, bough, spew,
intuitive, spew, opal, acquiesce,
true, truth, gamble, watermelon, spew, malevolent,
genuine, opal, spew, spew, mellifluous

II. Someone Whom You Want to Seduce

whisk, plot, lamb, south, opal, ubiquitous

III. (Conceivably) the "One"

opal,
bread,
luminescent,
primordial, bloodstone,
quick, opal, apropos,
pseudonym,
opal, ethyl,
malaise, mule, murder,
liminal, mellifluous,
impresario, embroil, opal, spew,
implacable,
imbue, Louvre, wiggle, loud, allow

IV. Someone to and with Whom You Will Never Belong

west, hope, loop,
fortuitous, ebb, opal, ebb,
mellifluous, acouasm, ebb, please,
where, why, mellifluous,
go, go, go,
opal, no, joy, spew, yow, watch,
close, powder, wish,
wish, loud, lose, loud, mellifluous,
wherewithal, platoon, platitude, fallow

The Asthmatic Boy Gains the Skill of Sunbreath

The asthmatic boy is the one who loves you,
who knows the aureate taste of a breath
but drips into your mouth its honey relentlessly.

His withered lungs savor air,
know that even fickle things need love
and can be essential to survival.

There were always times he couldn't breathe,
but his honeydew-half chest now rots daily,
bears fruit again, then rots anew.

Set us on fire, his lungs say,
we know how to be without air.
Perhaps this is the right way to deal with rot.

Perhaps he needs another pair of lips,
something that will let him breathe again
the way you did, or at least will incinerate.

Every time he kissed you,
there were lanterns in your mouth
bubbling up from your molten gold heart,

and he could breathe,
oh god, how he could breathe,
paper lanterns incandescent,

drag of light expanding
past membrane (he could see,
oh god, how he could see).

His dark lungs sprouted constellations,
and he wants to blot them out,
but stars burn for lifetimes.

Perhaps this isn't the first lifetime,
and this smoldering rot has always been
and always will be for eons, sweet,

but he will breathe fire with or without you,
scorching new lines between stars
in his galactic, airless lungs.

The Asthmatic Boy Learns to Breathe Underwater

The asthmatic boy swims
in the community pool,

knows how not to breathe,
how to keep things to himself

alone in the water.
The sun is tired of giving

for the day; the water relaxes,
slow, into indigo.

The asthmatic boy finds,
quick, the end of his breath,

but he is alone in the water.
This is not an emergency.

He savors the churn
of the water like a heartbeat.

No one can hear him,
and he can hear no one.

This is the way he likes it,
the way he will always like it.

On the surface, the asthmatic boy
has no choice about breathing.

Here, he gives exhale
only when he wants to.

Here, at the end of his breath,
he wishes to be able.

Here, the water gives
the end of his breath back.

The Boy Learns to Transmute Flesh into Metal

Holiness is the distillation of forever,
and therefore, about the dense new flesh
of the infinitely regenerating heart
is an aura of something approximately divine.
True to form, ingestion is possible
but not ownership. Bring sacrifice:
agile hands doing as they please,
teeth planted like seeds in the heart-owner's lip,
empty stomach like a singularity.

This is the taste of an infinitely regenerating heart:
unprocessed cocoa, powdered red chili, ancient pharaoh honey.
Offer the heart's owner reprieve
from sentience, a chance to be sensation
wrapped in naked skin, offer
prayer and chemicals on an altar
like a cutting board, peel and flay
the heart like a lychee
and feast,
then watch its owner peel and flay himself for you.

Come up, blood saccharine
and spilling over lips to see
the heart just as you left it,
if not a little larger,
a little denser, a little more lustrous.

The Boy with a Sledgehammer for a Heart

One morning, you will wake up believing everything
the boy with a sledgehammer for a heart told you.
Among limes and flavored smoke,
you will wonder why it took you so long to love yourself,
why it feels like you need the boy you're with demolished,
and where all the goddamn mint in the world went.
The boy with a sledgehammer for a heart will have been muddling
all of it with his heart's handle at the bottom of the Earth.
Hephaestus' cantaloupe rind callouses grip the heart,
an unwieldy thing for most, but not for a god.
This is a fitting destiny, as the boy's heart always bloomed
as a weapon and a maker of weapons. He doesn't mind
its secondary use as a muddler if it lets him forget
and makes you remember that you don't know where he's gone.
You will have to try and recall the last mojito you had,
now the last mojito you *ever* had.
He didn't want to take that away from you,
but there were a lot of things he hadn't wanted:
to be left behind, to move to Olympus,
to learn so many horrifying skills:
patience, the fear of daybreak,
how to hold on while letting go.
He fits in well with the gods.

His heart is a good sledgehammer, nearly infinitely durable.
You gave him the power and knowledge of that power,
enchanting him in the slowest fire.
For this reason, Thor has sent him love letters,
entreating him with quick words to wait for Ragnarok in bed
with a real lightning god. The boy with a sledgehammer for a heart
never liked the metallic taste of plasma, never even kissed Zeus,
but he loves the romance of the Norse gods,
the morbid acceptance of a known future,
everything, especially evil, set free at the end of days.

He writes back only to Mjolnir.
He thinks perhaps only another mythical hammer will understand
how he feels, and it does, but Mjolnir only writes
how the boy will no longer need to pulverize mint
if he moves to Asgard. They have real love for hammers there.
The Greek gods say they love him more, would die if he left.
The boy doesn't know what anyone means by that anymore
because no one knows what they mean by it, not really.
He doesn't know if he wants to be away from the mint—or Persephone.
He doesn't love Persephone, but she crushes entire pomegranates
into his mouth and fucks him hard afterward.
She tastes like you do: oblivion, citrus, and spring.
Out of the overflow of the heart, the tongue wreaks
havoc. Hades enjoys havoc, likes the boy's spark.
The gods like to joke that blizzards happen
when the boy goes down on Persephone.
He likes being part of origin myths,
so she tries to earn his love by keeping any mint from growing,
and the boy with a sledgehammer for a heart bears
his heart like a cross with him to bed.

Cure for Chronic Childish

You're gonna carry that weight.
—Cowboy Bebop

Apply to be a colonist on Mars.
In the ten years before you go,
spend as much time as you can underwater.
Get used to knowing you could suffocate at any time.

With the little time you spend on land, feel
the gravity traveling from your scapulae
down your spine into the earthy blades
of your legs, along the twist of sinew
and into the ground. Memorize it.

Try to overcome it on your own
by standing on roofs, climbing mountains,
jumping out of airplanes. (Is it working?)
Try to carry someone else's weight.
(What about now?) Carry it
for as long as possible. (Now?

Hahaha. Look how much water it takes
to float even your inconsequential weight.
And during lift off to Mars, appreciate the immense
amount of energy required to help the dust-speck
that is your body escape Earth's gravity.

This is how you'll grow up—weightless
and knowing in the fabric of your desmosomes
how incapable you are.)

Cure for Someone Else's Definition of Masculinity

Approach the glass box inside you
where that atrophied splinter of flesh
remains comatose, sedated by society
or whatever you want to blame.
Knock, and it will wake up like a fish
that has waited its whole life to be fed.
Imagine yourself a swan made of star stuff
as you warm the glass against your body
to melt it and free that part of you, now
dancing into the form of a young girl
(she'll be eight years old at most;
you've stunted her growth so much).
Cut a swath from your blue cloth-walls,
and note how the paint peels to reveal violet.
Make a sundress to the girl's specifications
(her specifications are, after all, yours),
and study her dancing, the inimitable twirl
of a reawakened galaxy in her skirt frills.
Cut more cloth and make her a bed
so you can tuck her in when she's done.
Come back the next day and the next (and the next).
Feed her with the hydrogen and deuterium
leaking from the new holes in your cloth-walls.
She'll burn it all to helium-knowledge. When she's grown,

fall in love with a bisexual girl.
She need not love you back,
but she must want something from you,
and you must want more than anything
to give it to her. Agree to meet inside you
on a night when the air smells of a beach
on the moon. Do not apologize for the holes
in your walls. Introduce her to the you
that has outgrown her one sundress.

Your lover didn't know it,
but this is what she wants from you.
Use this room inside you. Use the bed you made.
Use what you learned about making your body
something marvelous, magnanimous, galactic.

Cure for the Post-grad Blues (The Coral Springs Survival Guide)

I.

There is none.[1]
The common name of this disease
is "existential dread."

A pretty human being may help.
Create a space for them
in which they need not prove anything.
Taste, then, how they birth stars in your mouth
and thunderstorms in a secret place.
Even in the plethora of moments you do not want to be loved,
they will love you.[2]

You must choke their synapses with dopamine.[3]
Blind every other sense
with a (3 hour) kiss to the clitoris.
Laugh at the masses,
those who pursue sex
for pleasure or love.
To visit oblivion for a moment—
this is as close to a cure as you will get.

II. Addendum

Everything is always breaking.
Bonds break,[4] news breaks, ground breaks,[5]
floodgates break, clocks break, skin breaks.[6]
But the sky also breaks,
and so do floodgates and ground.[7]

You must decide
love and lightning
is a false dichotomy,

no need for Aphrodite *and* Zeus.
(The Norse are a touch closer,
as Love[8] gives birth to Thor,
but it is still not good enough.)

This new god must reign over
electricity, Ben Franklin, neurons,
pain, faith.
This new god must have no gender;
Thor and Zeus and FPL lack the finesse
of an axon or a neurotransmitter.
This new god of the liminal
must head a new pantheon,
standing next to outer space,
who is perhaps their eldest sister;
flight, their baby brother;
and quantum mechanics, their mother.

You may hire Yahweh and Buddha as consultants
(but not one without the other),
since these are, after all, new gods.
Buddha will have them fast
on Jupiter to know detachment and its limits,[9]
and Yahweh will have them slaughter
one lamb each to know forgiveness and its price.[10]

----

1. This poem is not a guide.

2. This stanza of the cure is based on the case study of B[rest of name redacted]. It is hitherto unknown if her case is representative or if she is merely exceptional. The researcher suspects both. In support of the former, however, the researcher offers the difference between electricity in a laboratory and lightning in a hurricane. (And for this part of the cure to remain effective, it is imperative that you remember this crucial fact of physics: no form of electricity can make a home.)

3. Please refer to James Joyce's love letters to Nora for inspiration, particularly the second paragraph of one dated 8 December 1909.

4. Mostly chemical and emotional, though the latter more than the former.

5. Mostly physical—earthquakes and capitalist building projects. Figurative ground breaking is not a valid interpretation at this point.

6. Hearts, too, if you insist.

7. Figurative ground breaking is a welcome interpretation here.

8. That is, Frigg, from the Proto-Indo-European root, *pri-*, "to love."

9. That is, of course, unless you have a proclivity toward Deism, which is not a recommended belief system with this cure. Why create new gods if they are just going to leave? Please consult your shaman before attempting this cure.

10. "And if he bring a lamb for a sin offering, he shall bring it a female without blemish. And he shall lay his hand upon the head of the sin offering, and slay it for a sin offering in the place where they kill the burnt offering. And the priest shall take of the blood of the sin offering with his finger, and put it upon the horns of the altar of burnt offering, and shall pour out all the blood thereof at the bottom of the altar: And he shall take away all the fat thereof, as the fat of the lamb is taken away from the sacrifice of the peace offerings; and the priest shall burn them upon the altar, according to the offerings made by fire unto the Lord: and the priest shall make an atonement for his sin that he hath committed, and it shall be forgiven him" (Leviticus 4:32-35, KJV).

Cure for Several Ailments, Including Perhaps Loneliness

Let an introvert love you.
She need not be pretty or kind.
She need not even be warm.
She must, however, sing
bioluminescence in moth form, sing
inherence as the wings leave her mouth.

Before or after you make love,
rest your head on her narrow
bare back as she lies there,
head turned away from you.
If you think she hates you,
good—it's true and it is better
for you.
            You will try to suck the glow
from her lips during the act,
but when you look at yourself stark
naked in the mirror afterward,
you will see your firefly abdomen fade.
The problem is the same as it was
            when you were young:
nothing lives in a jar for long.

When you first feel that you have no more
for her to take, let her keep taking.
When you realize you still have more
for her to take, let her keep taking.
When you again and again feel that you have no more
for her to take, let her keep taking,
until you are always burning a hole
in the floor of you, and you find,
all the way at the bottom,
your own open cocoons.

Every Time You Try to Live in the Sea, You End Up Back on the Shore

She gives you a propeller. You savor the weight of it, the way it takes shoulder-back and arm to bear, the way the wood knuckles against spine, reminding you how close to touch bone really is. You try being a submarine, but even with the propeller you can't breathe underwater, and the wood rots.

She gives you a propeller. She says you deserve more, says you deserve steel, a whole airplane to fly you over the sea, but it's all she has (and herself, but God knows she won't give you this). God knows that really you only want gills.

She gives you a propeller. You stare at it in the sand. The shivering of the calf-muscle burn below your knees reminds you how long you've been trying not to sink into the coast. Soon, those calves disintegrate and the propeller beats you into shore like a blender.

She gives you a propeller. She always gives you a propeller. All you know now is how to receive one. Does anyone know how to receive a propeller, much less live in the sea? Certainly not you, not her, nor anyone you know. You give her a propeller.

Dokkaebi:Genesis//Exodus

You are born one night in a humid corner of the world from a bloodied toy hammer. Now and again, as you grow up in the woods, you hear crying near the glen where you make your bed. Imbued somehow with a curious reverence for sadness from your natal blood, you go to her. Whoever she is (for she is always someone new), her heart always seems a different shape of treasure (whether it is treasure or not). Imbued somehow with another, misguided reverence, you want her to see the treasure.

When something of her lachrymose reaches the soil, you can feel your home—the palms, the roots, the beetles—perennializing on the potassium, the manganese. She never knows why she is crying, sometimes denies it even while the forest feeds and grows. When you ask if she is hungry, the same denial—and the same evident truth. You can see her stomach as empty as an atom.

You ask if she will love you, and no matter what she says, she will—in her own way.

In exchange, you summon her a house. She sits by the fireplace while you put on a pot of soup. You are the soup. You are pork broth and rosemary and cayenne. You pour yourself out, strain your sledgehammer heart from the stock. "I love this," she says. "Let me eat your heart." You tell her it's too much if indeed she isn't hungry. "Let me eat your heart," she says. You tell her she doesn't know what she's asking.

"Let me eat your heart."

You pour your heart into her bowl. With her knife of a tongue, she stabs, scoops your heart, swift, into her throat. She doesn't taste. She swallows you whole. When she is done, she puts out the fire, asks to take to bed with you. In the languid wet of night, you hand yourself over out of reverence or boredom (you're never sure), and the moon slicks your bodies with a holy, demonic light. In death, you cry out for a tongue that will taste you as you ought to be tasted, a tongue that will ask if you are hungry.

When you awaken, she remains. Sometimes she remains long enough to become hungry again and again; sometimes she remains only long enough for you to watch her leave, when she takes the house with her (no longer imbued with any magic once it leaves the glen) without ever seeing a sliver of gold. In the empty lot, you plant seeds of a new heart (for the next will surely need to eat).

When you put on a pot of soup for the next traveler, you close your eyes, pretend the sound of your boiling heart drowns out the cries of every human in the forest with a sledgehammer in their stomach.

Lex Bobrow is a graduate of the University of Miami creative writing program and lives in south Florida with and near his loved ones. A writer by day and a writer by night, he loves a well-crafted cartoon and kisses so potent they warp the fabric of space-time.

In 20 years, you'll find him hiding in the Alcázar of Seville, scribbling love notes to gravity and the way she bites her lip, or in the Florida Keys kayaking through the mangroves where he makes his home. Perhaps he'll have a vacation cottage on the moon, but the ocean, the ocean will always call him back until he really does go home. Bury him in a garden by the Atlantic Ocean with a perpetual music box on his gravestone.

Lex is the winner of the 2012 Laurence Donovan Prize in Poetry, and you can find his work in *Mangrove Literary Journal, Black Heart Magazine, Maudlin House, Hermeneutic Chaos, Wingbeats II: Exercises and Practice in Poetry, Literary Sexts: A Collection of Short & Sexy Love Poems Vol I*, and a few other magazines.